For Eilish,

For the times that have been and the times to be.

ACKNOWLEDGMENTS

Certain of these poems appeared in the following magazines:

Acumen (UK), *Agenda* (UK), *American Poetry Monthly, The American Reporter, Aspect, California Quarterly, Candelabrum* (UK), *Coastlines, Connecticut River Review, Cumberland Poetry Review, Drastic Measures, Electric Acorn* (Eire), *The Epigrammatist, Envoi* (UK), *First Things, The Formalist, The Great Midwestern Poetry Quarterly, Hawaii Review, Hellas, Illuminations* (UK), *Iambs and Trochees, International Poetry Review, The Journal* (UK), *Kansas Quarterly, Krax* (UK), *The Laurel Review, Legal Studies Forum, Light Quarterly, The New Formalist, The North Stone Review, Other Poetry* (UK), *Outposts Poetry Quarterly* (UK), *Pacific Ocean Review* (NZ), *Pacific Review, Poem, Poet* (India), *Poetry Greece, Poetry Magazine, Poetry Monthly* (UK), *Poetry Overview, Ltd, The Raintown Review, Revival* (Eire), *River City, Sequoia, Slant, South* (UK), *The Southern Review, Spirit, Stone Country, Sun Temples, The Tennessee Quarterly, Voice and Verse* (UK), *and The Wisconsin Review.*

Certain of these poems appeared in the following anthologies:

Literature and its Writers (Bedford/St. Martin's Press, NY 2006), *Off the Record* (LSJ Publications, Indianapolis, 2004), *Good Poems* (Viking Penguin, New York, 2002), *Only Morning in her Shoes* (U. of Utah Press, Logan, 1994), *In the West of Ireland* (Enright House, Dromlought, 1992), *California Poets Anthology* (California State Poetry Society, San Francisco, 1986).

Also, certain of these poems were published in *Another Bloomsday at Molly Malone's Pub* (The Inevitable Press, Laguna

My Dark People

by T.S. Kerrigan

Centı

Central Ave. Press 8400 Menaul Blvd. NE Suite A #211
Albuquerque, NM 87112

ISBN: 978-0-9798452-0-8

Library of Congress Cataloging-in-Publication Data

Kerrigan, T. S.
My dark people / by T.S. Kerrigan.
p. cm.
ISBN 978-0-9798452-0-8
I. Title.

PS3611.E7638M9 2008
811'.6--dc22

2008001979

Central Ave. Press
8400 Menaul Blvd. NE Suite A #211
Albuquerque, NM 87112

www.centralavepress.com

Printed in the United States of America

Beach, 1999), and in *The Shadow Sonnets and Other Poems* (The Scienter Press, Louisville, 2006).

Several of these poems were read by the author on the California Artists Radio Theater production of *Strolling with the Poets* for National Public Radio in 2002.

Finally, some of these poems were issued on-line by *The New Formalist* as an e-book entitled *Conversations in the Dark at the Winter Solstice* in 2005 and on the website, *The Hyper Texts,* in the same year.

Contents

Consolations **81**

I

Awakenings

Children lose their way in dreams,
Never knowing where to turn,
What condemns and what redeems.

On Rosses Point

The shadowed moon invests the shore,
Woman of roses, long black hair;
I gently knock outside your door.

I come to take your captain's place,
Who gusts have borne far out to sea;
You drown me in a surf of lace.

Lie back with me till morning tide,
When light is dim along the coast,
And rest, like Eve, at Adam's side.

Then watch the circling sky unwind,
Embracing us in early light,
As though we two were all mankind.

I'll stay until the night is done,
Woman of roses, long black hair,
To find your mouth in moon, in sun.

The Aria My Mother Sang

Her slender fingers struck the keys.
L'amour est un oiseau rebelle,
She sang in that soprano voice
Like some flirtatious femme fatale.

I've heard that voice again in dreams
Through all the intervening years,
And once at night on some boreen
In rural Sligo years ago.

She played when neighbors rose to sing:
"The Minstrel Boy," "Old Folks at Home,"
"I'll Take you Home again, Kathleen,"
(My specialty: "Don't Fence Me In").

My father sat behind the crowd
And never sang a bar, so ill
At ease, he'd often leave to smoke
A cigarette and disappear.

(I heard his failing steps resound
Across the hall the night she died,
His grief so unendurable,
He wept each time we spoke her name).

An understanding, unexpressed,
Informed their lives. I can't recall
A soulful kiss, a bold embrace,
And yet I rarely saw them fight.

L'amour est un oiseau rebelle.
What wantonness her voice possessed.
But was it operatic show
Or simply passion manifest?

Dream Women

They were never quite what he expected,
Those women he dreamed into existence;
If he imagined them as fair, they were dark,
If he envisioned them as willful, they were submissive;
If child-like, they proved calculating.

Resisting the world of his making,
Fashioned in those hours of dreaming,
These women he formed in his mind
Subverted the landscape of his creation
With maps of their own devising.

He lay awake as they were sleeping,
Lamenting his failed conception.
How do we live at all but in our dreams?
But the dream is not fitted to the dreamer,
The dreamer is fitted to the dream.

Magdalene

Aware her power belongs to night
(The moon ascendant, day dispersed),
She dreads impending rays of light,

Confounding all her spells and charms
To quell the god, preserve the man
who holds her nightly in his arms.

To keep resurgent dawn away,
She tries to nail the shutters closed,
She draws the bolts against the day.

But planes of light in morning skies
Transcend her patchwork barriers,
Rekindling visions in his eyes.

Restored as god and man once more
(The sun ascendant, night dispersed),
He leaves her, standing by the door,

To ponder things she can't possess,
The glimmer of the moon and stars,
The summer's scent, the wind's caress.

Give Me That Old Time Coition

I

When Bea Shapiro walked to school,
Enamored like that Nazarene
Who gave his heart to Magdalene,
I strayed behind, a tongue-tied fool.

I'd catch her eyes sometimes in class,
and looked away before she guessed
I dreamt of splendor in the grass.

Though Boaz may have bragged of Ruth,
My phoenix cast a brighter light.
Believe me, that's the gospel truth.

And when she smiled I didn't care
That Xerxes lay in Esther's arms
Or Soloman knew Sheba's charms,
I loved a creature far more fair.

The fifties proved repressive times;
The Pentateuch, unnatural law
Made simple joys egregious crimes.

II

But Vico says that destiny,
That ever turning cosmic wheel
Evolves in cycles none can see.

We felt a new decade begin,
When lovers lay in fields of flowers
As fragrant as those ancient bowers,
Their ecstasy no longer sin.

The year before I bought a car
She ran off with some local *mensch*
And made me love her from afar.

A girl I never got to kiss,
And now would never be my bride,
became my Jewish Beatrice.

Alone, I cursed the stars, the moon,
The firmament, all womankind,
And all the planets unaligned,
That I'd been born too late, too soon.

The Muslin Dress

The Sunday train to Abbeyfeale
Came clattering past stacks of hay,
The prickly gorse and Hawthorn rows,
Brought home a girl too long away.

The band played Kerry polkas late
That night at Tommy Tobin's place.
The moment she walked through the door,
The color rose in each lad's face.

We watched her move across the room,
The scarlet muslin dress she chose
Revealing long and shapely legs.
We'd rarely seen the likes of those.

And, oh, we thought, to be the man
Of all who danced with her before
To hold her in our arms that night,
A heap of muslin on the floor.

Land's End

I pause along these sandstone cliffs
Where Garryowen stops to smell
A heap of Eucalyptus leaves,
And think of those seafaring men
On islands lying south of here,

Those Polynesians, ages past,
Who navigated miles of sea
In fleets of flimsy hand-hewn craft,
Without a compass, gyroscope,
By rhythms of the earth and sky.

Invested with that knowledge once,
What made us break the pagan link
With earth, make blind the hidden eye?
Was erring mankind dispossessed?
Were we cast from the garden twice?

Pacific Palisades

My Dark People

Invoking a wrathful God
With candles, icons, beads,
The liturgy of the middle ages,

My dark people clutched
Faith like a crucifix,
The grim descendants of a tribe

Hardened by famine and plague,
That bullied, burned and killed
In the old blackguard days,

Knew the grief and shame
Of the heartbreak fields,
The hunger and want of winter.

Schooled in the pubs, they clothed
An insult in the guise of praise,
Praise in the guise of an insult.

Reared in the impenitent rage
Of my forefathers' blood,
I am Tomás Ó Ciaragáin.

Be wary lover, stranger,
We emerged in a black hour,
Our legacy: a blessing and a curse.

Mornings in Sligo

I
Strandhill

Manannan mac Lir
Drifts like a grey cloud
Along this west of Ireland coast,

The crones of Sligo say,
His voice in the rising wind
Muttering black spells,

Troubling the blood's memory
With dreams of furious storms,
The wreckage on far shores.

I imagine him on solitary rocks,
Gauging the tide's movements,
And the moon's pale changes,

Urging the white-headed
Stallions of the black Atlantic
Hard on this peaceful strand.

II
Maugherow

I remember an icy wind
Giving querulous tongues
To ash, oak, and willow
those mornings in Maugherow,

The sweep of her brown hair
Across a white pillow,
The scant outline of her breasts
Beneath grey linen.

I remember, out our window,
Queen Anne's Lace
Blown on a ruined stile
At the edge of Donal's field,

The black and white cattle
Like ghosts in the first light,
Our two bodies merging
In a wild tangle of bedding.

Drays and Lorries, Hackneys, Traps

(James Joyce's father reflects on the past on the morning of his son's last day in Dublin.)

I

Those drays and lorries, hackneys, traps
Outside my windy stool again,
That clattering of wheels on stone.
We wait for suns to rise, to set,
For someone to be born, to die.

"Now Poppie, put the kettle on.
Where's Jim Aroo, that layabout?"
The dreams that boyeaux weaves at night!
Young fallows ought to seize the die.
It's only hoors get kip in bed.

My bride (the havens be her rest),
Appends to me in dreams, that sweet
Compaction both the lolly, rose,
My dearest angel culled to God.
But cures for grief are under heel.

We'll have her clandescending crowd,
Those counter-jumping chancers here.
What times, what murrains these!
To think I martyred into them.
That soul betraythal none forgave.

II

Christ, to hear the names he calls himself,
Seamustephanosdedalus,
A familiar of every alley, lane,
Every stick and stone,
Of this grey as lamestone town.

Forever at his holy alls,
He'll cadge a dross of craythur
Between the dusk and morning hoors,
Play Adam to Evening every night
In Monto, Monto, Monto town.

Given the finest edification, I saw
To that, put me to the pin of my collar,
As if who killed bloody Caesar was more
Important than who killed Cock Robin.

Suppose he means to disown us all now,
Seed, breed, and generation.

Well, he shouldn't expect to see my face
If he returns, I'll be the next to go
The way of all fools, go off
To the place they say partings are unknown.

III

O, let them talk of gargle, hoors,
Those Paddy Thinks and Mickey Munds,
Afflict the ways of worldly mien.
To think I'd sink as low as this,
Be pinchioned off at half my pay

And end, this sad protenditor
Who fell beside his martyred Chief,
No sooner calved then licketh, haith.
And who'll put Humpty up again?
That pack of huns that dragged him down?

Jim's always been the spate of me.
He won't forget who brogued him here.
The pair of us, if troth be told,
Have always been one blood, one bone.
"You hear me girl? One blood, one bone."

"Christ Poppie, where's my bloody tea.
I'll have it yet, you slack-jawed girl.
Don't cod me now, I want the true
And proper oracle, bogwater black.
You hear me, girl, bogwater black."

Elegy for the Young Who Fell in Unpopular Causes

Those young who fashion now disdains,
Deceived by what they heard and saw,
Were sent away on failed campaigns.

Who swaddled them in stars and stripes,
Declined to teach them natural law?
Who forged their outworn archetypes?

Their ribbons, medals time disclaims,
Their brief renown the years withdraw.
Who still recalls their faces, names?

Interred in fields where cross shades cross,
Assessed by standards none foresaw,
Some future age may mourn their loss.

Those young, dispatched to fight a war,
Were sent to die untutored, raw.
Whose causes were they fighting for?

The Old Blatherskites Have Their Say, Bewailing the Younger Generation

Jem

Look at those boyos, the swaggering fools,
Lurching through life with their drugs and their drink,
Getting expelled from the National Schools,
Blaring their rock and roll, how do they think?
Why would their bed partners ever suppose
A gaudy tattoo and pierced ears and nose
Seem to the rest of us smart, debonair?
Why do they look like they're not really there?

Dosser

What will they do, become 9 to 5 boys
By snapping their fingers like that, the fools?
The future's no place for excuses and ploys,
Larking through life with your own set of rules.
They'll never see crooked places made straight
Or play at musical chairs with the great.
They'll learn soon enough they haven't a prayer.
Aren't they appalled people see them and stare?

Jem

How could their girls be appealing as wives,
The kittens lent to their friends on a whim?
How could their kind lead conventional lives?

Dosser

Imagine them parents, planned or unplanned,
Getting along with no money on hand,
Bathing the kiddies and combing their hair.
Why do they look like they don't really care?

Jem

Or are we just envious, priest-ridden men,
Browbeaten, bullied in chapel at ten?

Dosser

Rushed into marriage pre-penetration,
Purity mattering more than sensation.

Jem

Often pretentious, seldom sincere.

Dosser

Why do we look like we're not really here?

The Lost Children

Children lose their way in dreams,
Wandering the unmarked roads,
Wading through the braided streams.

All their fields of green recede,
Leaving them, at journey's end,
Autumn's waste of straw and seed.

Children sin against the breath;
Every muddled prayer they speak
Only brings them nearer death.

Winter scrawls in stem and leaf
All its scroll of prophecies,
Days of heartbreak, nights of grief.

Children lose their way in dreams,
Never knowing where to turn,
What condemns and what redeems.

Underground

Rest period in a school for "defectives."

At recess time, they're kept in class,
Their heads on desks, their eyelids closed.
Most listen, let the morning pass.
One boy, his purpose unsupposed,
Goes underground, discovers springs
And limpid crystals. Hid from day,
Among the dark's protective wings,
His burdened body slips away,
He dreams in that secluded place.
When roll is called, his fate is sealed,
They drag him forward in disgrace
To stand in front of class, revealed,
So horribly misshapen, odd,
He only dares appear to God.

Sleepwalker

For Elizabeth

Shadow daughter, you wander deep
In the improbable foliage of dreams tonight,
Past meridians beyond my knowing.

I try to envision those languid coasts,
Those luxuriant rainforests where you loiter,
The strange, luminous creatures you encounter,

Those secret destinations in the night,
Those far provinces I can never chart,
The terra incognita of the child.

Shadow daughter, I wake to the tread
Of your feet in the hall tonight, and rise
To clasp a clumsy hand on your shoulder.

Leading you back to your bed in darkness,
I envy you, weary from your journey, the fantastic
Shells and flowers you clutch in your hands.

The Long-Awaited Child

(Hilary Kerrigan, b. October 12, 1981)

Unmoored from cradling seas
(The sea within the womb,
The sea of night before),
Immersed in shadow, light,

What instinct set her course
Across those distant shoals,
The long-awaited child?

I hold her in my arms,
This night-engendered girl,
The spindrift of those seas
Resplendent in her eyes.

What longing made her seek
This harborage of dawn,
The long-awaited child?

The Bridge to America

For Joe Kennedy

On board the rotting coffin ships
They fingered icons, beads,
Invoked the Sacred Heart of Christ,

Our Irish forebears, proud in rags
With mouths of crooked teeth,
The meek who dared inherit earth.

Unmoved by intimations scrawled
Across prophetic winds,
They sought the solitude of stars.

At last a landfall came in view,
A dark expanse of coast,
This brooding New Hibernia.

I picture them on rundown wharfs,
The greenhorns striking out
For Canaans all across the land.

Pretenders to the windfall night,
The vast unchosen staked their claims,
The meek who dared inherit earth.

II
Transgressions

Our nonchalant neglect of those we love,
Our catalogue of small atrocities,
Consign us to this sleepless world of grey.

The Jargon of Lovers

The jargon of lovers has no word for absence.

With her image only a blur in my mind,
I was certain my blackest hours had passed.
They'd never catch me staring into space again.

But a snatch of music, the *Valse des Fleurs*,
Playing over and over in my head,
Had me twisting in my sleep last night.

By morning the immodest fragrance of jasmine
(Reminiscent of the perfume she always wore)
Came flooding through the white billowing curtains.

As I moved like a stranger in the awakening streets,
I encountered her lips on every woman's face,
Littering the morning like rose petals.

The jargon of lovers has no word for regret,
No names for the lonely stations of memory.

Be Thankful, Unicorn

Be thankful, Unicorn,
Your kind does not exist.

Chimera, Cyclops, Witch,
Your terrors live in dreams
An ancient mind conceived.
We wake to darker themes.

Be grateful, Basilisk,
Your sort was never born.

Behemoth, Dragon, Sphinx,
Be happy you're ideal.
These times engender forms
More terrible, more real.

Kincarrie Miller

A sickly girl, we took her in that spring
When I was ten, my brother twelve,
Another of my mother's strays. It seems
Her salesman father had to leave
On business trips from time to time.

They'd moved into the neighborhood, the wife
And mother's absence unexplained,
Some months before. Though just fifteen, disease
Had culled the roses from Kincarrie's face
And left her eyelids purple veined.

She seemed content to share a room with boys,
Read novels, spoke a little French,
And looking down her spectacles, disdained
Our "bourgeois" neighborhood, where none, she learned,
Read Gide, Hugo, de Maupassant.

One night while sprawled across an upper bunk
My eyes strayed from my grammar book.
I saw her, having brushed her teeth and hair,
Emerge in bra and panties, sans her robe,
Still drying on the backyard line.

Impulsively, I doused the light, jumped down,
And clasped her body close to me,
My skinny, trembling hands around her waist,
My throbbing face between her girlish breasts.
"What's going on?" my brother yelled.

I instantly released her unresisting form,
Aware her eyes were fixed on me.
My brother rose and turned the light back on.
I stared at him but uttered no response.
I didn't understand myself.

I flicked the light off two more times that night.
She looked at me as though her eyes
Had never really seen my face before.
My brother, angry, knocked me down and made
Me cry. "What's wrong with you," he screamed.

That fall her father got a job up north.
I watched the Bekins moving van
Depart with all their worldly goods inside
And thought of how her fragile body felt
That night while gathered in my arms.

My fourteenth spring a voice outside
My bedroom door awakened me,
I heard enough to know Kincarrie died.
"She never got the proper care," my aunt
Exclaimed. I couldn't get to sleep that night.

So set apart by circumstance, did she
Accept my boyish lust that night?
Would other arms encircle her? Or was
I last to draw that pallid body close
Before the cold embrace of earth?

Childhood Memories of a War: Living Among the Casualties

After the hostilities, the men with missing limbs
Showed up in all the public places,
As traumatized families, seeing
Them on streets and in parks, complained
Of a bureaucratic oversight.

Recipients of negligible benefits from the nation,
Their astounding numbers were impossible to ignore.
They sold us papers on street corners,
Or offered to shine our shoes for a quarter,
If we could only bear to look them in the eyes.

(It was easier watching the paraplegics
Play listless basketball
Games on makeshift courts,
Though we all soon grew tired
Of the noise of clanging wheelchairs.)

When they were mercifully removed to veterans hospitals
And nursing homes, as agreed behind
Closed doors, it was for the common good.
Confronted daily with these grotesque casualties,
How were we to forget the terrible effects of war?

Claire

I

He'll see a woman pass, and swear,
The way her body moves, it's Claire.
But every time he calls her name,
It's just a nurse from down the hall,
A woman not like Claire at all.

II

They'd gone out dancing, had some beer
That week they shipped him off to war,
She'd talked about a stage career.

He read her notes out there each day,
That desert half a world away.

He wrote her back, described the wind,
That wind that overtakes the land
The way it overtakes the mind.

He never did get through to her
That few come back the men they were.

III

Claire's newest film came out last May.
They showed it in the ward today.
He watched, but never said a word.
She grows more lovely frame by frame,
The girl he lost and can't reclaim.

Secretly Reading the Stories in my Mother's Magazines

We had very few books, and no library near
Our old ramshackle house at the end of the street
In that neighborhood stinking of cabbage and beer.

So I savored the love lives of Allison, Dawn,
All those Merediths, Ericas, Tiffanies, Brookes,
In my bedroom upstairs or the chaise on the lawn,

Though on greater reflection those names seemed as queer
As *souffle de poisson or escalopes de veau,*
In a neighborhood stinking of cabbage and beer.

And I thought to myself as I read more and more,
I might find that oasis of beauty and grace
And encounter those females I'd grown to adore.

But the dawning of truth proved my night of despair.
I'd been lied to, defrauded, seduced and betrayed
Like some pitiful character out of Flaubert.

With my dreams turned to dust, my dilemma was clear:
I was trapped in a world full of Marys and Anns
In a neighborhood stinking of cabbage and beer.

Roger Kelley

They placed us alphabetically
In history and math;
You sat between Bob Katz and me.

You'd been expelled from other schools
For truancy and theft,
And bragged you'd broken all the rules.

By spring we heard you faced arrest
For unpaid traffic fines;
Your brand new Ford was repossessed.

It's ages since we saw your face
Or read your name in print,
But who'd forget that time and place?

The week they took the Ford away,
To get to Mexico,
You panicked, stole a Chevrolet.

The owner tried to intervene,
A teacher from the school.
You shot her twice and fled the scene.

The day I read they gave you life,
I swore I'd rather die
Than live without a girl or wife.

Yet even grief wears off at last.
We spoke about you less
And less, forgot about the past.

But social workers called one day
To see Bob Katz and me,
Then shook their heads and went away.

You named us each your closest friend,
Two kids you swore to them
"support you to the very end,"

Acquaintances you'd only met
Because of happenstance,
Contingent on the alphabet.

Elvis Kissed Me

"Elvis kissed me once," she swears,
Sitting in a neon dive,
Ordering her drinks in pairs.

Two stools down you nurse a beer,
Sensing easy pickings here.

"Back in sixty-eight," she sighs,
Smoothing back her yellow hair.
Black mascara smears her eyes.

Drawing near, you claim you've met,
Offer her a cigarette.

"Call me cheap," she sobs, "or bad,
Say that decent men dismissed me,
Say I've lost my looks, but add,
Elvis kissed me."

My Father's Keys

He couldn't name a single door
He opened with this set of keys
We came across the year he died.

A son in some old parable,
I clutch them in my hands tonight.

He never hoped to see again
Those rooms he entered years ago,
Except through recollection's eye.

But time, which always takes its tithes,
Had blurred those scenes beyond recall.

His memory had lost its way
Among those darkened corridors
Where every turning looked the same.

I think of him again tonight
With all his songs and laughter stilled,

And clutch them in my hands once more,
These artifacts he left behind,
These emblems of his passages.

Diversions

She was passing my chair
To attend to some mums
In a porcelain vase,

When her fingertips strayed
For a second or two
On my shoulders and neck.

With a shudder inside,
I glanced up from my book,
Though our eyes never met.

With the mums all arranged,
She was off to the town
In a train of Cologne.

But the rest of the day,
With the book put aside,
I relived each caress,

Those diversions of love,
She'd forgotten about
In the moment she passed.

License

They wander down in search of food each year
When summer turns the higher meadows brown,
Those ragged herds of starving spotted deer.
One August afternoon, come back from town,
I saw, beside my fence, a grazing doe.
I grabbed my rifle, worked the bolt, and thought,
I bet she's eaten everything I grow.
I trained my weapon, nearly fired a shot,
Then watched her darting gracefully away,
A creature far too glorious to harm.
The doe would live to steal another day.
I slung the loaded rifle round my arm.
My neighbor saw, expressing disbelief
That beauty should give license to a thief.

Deceptions

That April, morning etched our room with light —
I still recall awaking — bleary eyed,
I told you all I dreamt about that night,
My turning, all those hours, from side to side.

I still recall awaking, bleary-eyed,
It all comes back, that dream of souls half dead,
My turning all those hours from side to side,
That silent, sad procession in my head.

It all comes back, that dream of souls half dead.
There's something else — I've tried but can't explain,
That silent, sad procession in my head,
We bore somehow their share of earthly pain.

There's something else — I've tried but can't explain.
You'll read these lines someday and then you'll know,
We bore somehow their share of earthly pain,
I knew it then and never told you so.

You'll read these lines someday and then you'll know,
I saw us both among those lost that night,
I knew it then and never told you so,
That April, morning etched our rooms in light.

Lines Written in the Small Hours of the Morning

It's not the silver opulence of light,
The showy circuitry of moon and stars
Awakens us at three o'clock each night,
Nor drunkards stumbling home from bars,
Nor eerie timbers creaking up above.
The years of friendship's unacknowledged pleas,
The nonchalant neglect of those we love,
Our catalogue of small atrocities,
Consign us to this sleepless world of grey,
To play earth's last survivors, left alone.
We wait for dawn. But why? To chase away
The memories we've labored to disown?
Or grasp for light before the dark descends
Into that final sleep that never ends?

The Berkeley Hills

Though scattered through a hundred towns,
Their college days long past them now,
I still can feel their presence here,
The girls we lured on autumn nights
Among these lonely, windswept hills.

Relentless winter sweeps away
The signatures our bodies etched
Between the scrub and chaparral,
In undergrowth that bears no trace
Of fleeting markings passion leaves.

When fall transforms these glades and woods,
What's etched for them in memory,
The faces of those fumbling boys
Who drew them down in darkness once
Among these lonely windswept hills?

Recessional

Our lives now pass in retrograde,
Our powers failing day by day,
The fools who wished a world remade.

We faced the future unafraid,
Ignored the signs that spoke decay.
Our lives now pass in retrograde.

The men we trusted most betrayed
Us, held us all within their sway,
The fools who wished a world remade.

We sensed too late the role they played,
The things they knew and didn't say.
Our lives now pass in retrograde.

The times disband the plans we laid
And casts our dreams in disarray,
The fools who wished a world remade,

Without a torch or map to aid
Our steps along this unmarked way.
Our lives now pass in retrograde,
The fools who wished a world remade.

9/11

Grimm Accounts

I

The old inconsequence of age: denied
My proper place and voice these latter days.
Who once received the unremitting praise
Of greater men, by lesser men decried;
My fortune nearly gone, and all my joy.
I thought my deeds, performed in countless ways,
Would like a beacon, keep my fame ablaze.
I've known the reputations men destroy.
Some cunning politicians now contend
I plundered Heaven, brought the wrath of God,
And some deny there ever was a stalk.
My pockets bare, without a bean to spend,
I drag another cow to fairs. How odd
To be so poor, so full of rambling talk.

II

She rang me up again last night,
Ostensibly about my book,
But talked at length about her plight.

Her husband slips away each year
But never tells her where he goes
Or even when he'll reappear.

I listened to her anguished voice,
Lamenting what her life's become
Because of one disastrous choice.

She still has plaits of golden hair,
What seems to some an ordered life,
A pair of daughters passing fair.

But all the while she waits in dread,
Her fingers twisting both her rings,
She'll feel his tug upon her head.

Villonesque

Mais ou sont les neiges d'antan?

I

Please tell me if you can, *mon frere*,
How all those former wantons fare:

The nymphets, teasers, schemers, flirts
Who always acted so demure
In midi, mini, maxi skirts;

Nicole, I met behind the stair
Who came to me sans underwear;

Gervais, I saw at break of day
Come scrambling through my window once,
A ghost in filmy lingerie.

And where, *mon frere*, does longing go?
In *billets-doux*, the cant of verse?

And what's become of last year's snow?

II

And where are all those Adelaides
Who smiled behind the balustrades?

The Angeliques of singles bars
In padded bras and clinging pants,
Who incandesced like falling stars?

And where's Marie, that font of bliss,
Who only gave me Tosca's kiss?

And Madeleine, the ingenue,
Who followed me around for days,
A man then pushing 42?

And where, *mon frere*, does passion go?
The silent grave? Oblivion?

And what's become of last year's snow?

Homage (of Sorts) to Michael Praetorius

The principal source for the idea of conflict in the concerto is Michael Praetorius

Palisca, Baroque Music

Michael Praetorius "knew"
(Great men intuit such things)
All he'd been taught was untrue.
Wasn't he moved to insist
Watching the Thirty Years War,
Music and strife coexist?
Scholars have said all along,
Etymologically viewed,
All his conclusions were wrong.
Still, one's inclined to declare,
Watching the usual gore,
Hearing a marche militaire,
Music's a cousin to war,
Just as Praetorius swore.

Love's Season

I offered a bouquet,
A dozen *Blanche Moreau,*
A rose our elders say
Appeared like drifts of snow
Through efflorescent May
In gardens long ago.
"But blossom, sepal, leaf,
May live a day and die,"
You said. "Is love as brief?"
You winced at my reply.
"Can passion ever slow
The cycles of the sky?
Suns nurture, overthrow.
It's only apropos
That roses live to die."

La Vie Boheme

Between heaven and hell they lived. . . .

Anthony Kerrigan, *Abode in Paris*

I

That summer in the Rue Jacob
I practiced on the Bechstein grand,
Franz Liszt, Chopin's nocturnes, etudes.
He wrote ballades and epigrams.
We lived on love and little else,
On cheap Bordeaux and *objets d'art.*

On Sundays we explored the Louvre:
Those halls of vibrant canvasses,
Poussin, Vermeer, Vouet, David.
One found in antiquarians
A gaze of undisguised hauteur.
A certain condescending glance

Defined the classic temperament,
Or, in the bust of Hadrian
Contemptuous averted eyes.
But Gericault and Delacroix
Transcended all, invoked in oils
The cause of human liberty.

II

We marveled at the cabarets,
The *douce-amere* of Piaf, Brel,
The savoir vive of Prevert's songs.
When students rose for *liberte,*
We joined them on the barricades.
We lived like artists, hour by hour,

But art and life are not the same,
One founders as the other thrives.
We quarreled about Napoleon,
Le Rouge et Noir, l'amour propre.
One drunken night he blacked both eyes.
I packed and left that life for good.

When, after almost twenty years,
Nostalgia brought me back to France,
The Paris that I once adored,
I crossed the *Pont du Carrousel,*
Found *Liberte*, her breasts exposed,
Resembling now a drab grisette.

The Ingenue

She'd heard the tales of both those girls
Who no one else on earth believed,
Those innocents in golden curls:
The startled princess by the sea
The taurine-headed god deceived,
Who gave herself to him for free,
And Leda, pale among the reeds,
Who felt his down against her skin
And satisfied his baser needs,
Too young to know the stain of sin.

Attending to those tales in full,
She vowed she'd never be misled
By providential bird or bull,
Or let such creatures share her bed.
But wily Zeus could always guess
The way to turn a pretty head.
Could riches bring her happiness?
Awakening to golden rain
Across her fallow nakedness,
Not even Danae dare complain.

The Queen

The gates of Sparta opened wide
To welcome back our errant queen,
Her withered husband by her side.

She hadn't shown her face in years,
But older men recalled her charms,
That peerless form, those pendent spheres.

We saw, instead, to our surprise,
A gnarled doll, a fingerling,
A gorgon of diminished size.

What king would burn a city now
To get her back again, this crone?
Was this a face to launch a skow?

We'd been misled by aging men,
Who saw with blinded Homer's eyes,
And dared proclaim this hag a ten.

Were wretched Paris still alive,
Who dared to judge the goddesses,
He'd readjust her score to five.

Rilke's Death

Milton died of blind ambition,
Robert Burns of heart disease,
Byron on a Grecian mission,
Keats of Scotch conspiracies,
Wordsworth died of inanition,
Shelley drowned in stormy seas,
Hardy in morose reflection,
Wilde by certain court decrees,
Swinburne in a grave condition,
Dylan by his "revelries."
Rilke's end exceeded those,
Showing beauty's blacker side;
Reaching out to touch a rose,
Pricked by thorns, he sickened, died.

Good Time Girls

In pushup bras and skintight jeans,
Those good time girls we knew in youth
All seemed to step from magazines,
Each body like a centerfold.
Voluptuaries bent on fun,
They proved to be as good as gold.

But beauty wasn't made to last;
It soon corrodes in smoke-filled bars,
Where none can reinvent the past.
The years move at a breathless pace,
Defying lotions, serums, creams,
Destroying beauty's form and face.

What's left for girls who time's undone,
Who never dreamed the laughs would end,
Then learn that they're no longer fun?
When men begin to grow unkind,
A good time girl just draws the shades
And tries to drink away her mind.

Conversations in the Dark at the Winter Solstice

In the midst of life we are in death.
Book of Common Prayer

My father rings again at four.
"Your mother's gone," he says.
"She's never run away before."

"I told you, Dad, the other day,"
I answer, half awake.
"She died last year in early May."

I sense once more his disbelief
Across the windblown wires,
And then, in increments, his grief,

Until a voice detached and dry,
A voice not his at all,
Is whispering a faint goodbye.

I tell myself, beware;
He's seen too much of night,
What night engenders there.

II

I put my father out of mind
And get to sleep again
Despite the constant growl of wind.

But then a daughter's downstairs cry
Awakens me at five.
She's dreamt she hurtles down the sky,

A sky so cold and lacking light
It preys upon our minds
For hours this longest winter's night.

I hold her closely, first of all,
As though these clumsy hands
Could somehow break her silent fall,

Then whisper, "Sleep," aware
She's seen too much of night,
What night engenders there.

Hollywood Boulevard: Christmas Eve

Go look for signs of Christmas here,
Among the glare of neon lights,

As runaways, strung out all day
in squalid rooms, all rise at dusk
And dredge the streets to buy or sell,

And prostitutes at Mann's Chinese
(Too young to purchase cigarettes),
Revolve like burnt out asteroids.

Go look for signs of Christmas here,
Along the transient Walk of Fame,

While biker gangs, secured a place
In local iconography,
Pass by on old Electra Glides,

And homeless couples go to sleep
In doorways, alleys, vacant lots,
Denied a room within the inn.

Go out, just as the Magi did
And seek a child among these lost,
Go find some signs of Christmas here.

On Golden Sands

I wait alone on golden sands
To hear the chapel bell strike ten,
Her sprightly step upon the stair,
That bird that flew into my hands,
To hold her closely once again.

Before the priest had caught her ear,
Described the metes and bounds of hell,
She spent a summer night with me,
Who now pretends she doesn't hear
The tolling of the chapel bell.

I know I'll catch no further sight
Of her out walking golden sands,
But who'd forget that face and form
That issued from the dark that night,
That bird that flew into my hands.

The Fall of a Lark

In memory of Nadia Anjuman, Afghani poet, reportedly beaten to death after publishing her first book of verse.

"My wings are closed...I cannot fly,"
You said before you plummeted,
A creature less of earth than sky.

What gift like yours endures for long,
Where ignorance throws lethal stones,
And bullies put an end to song?

No harbinger of harm or death
Can make a lark withhold its sound,
The bursts of that ecstatic breath.

You sang because you had to sing
(As well tell roses not to bloom),
Without a care for stone or sling.

But song remains an act of will.
You had to know instinctively
A singing bird's the first they kill.

The Girls of Halcyon Towns

Both lived provincial social lives
At Baptist picnics, county fairs,
The girls affecting country airs
Who farmers took as wives,
The jades with parasols,
Who chose to hone their female charms
In *fin de siecle* horsemen's arms
As soon as they'd outgrown their dolls.

Not one of all those girls conceived
That every idle step they made
Beyond that sheltered aspen glade
Could never be retrieved.
They went diverging ways,
Unmindful what the stars portend,
Or that our lives too often end
Ensnarled among our yesterdays,

But time, which takes so many shapes,
Dispatched them all to grey retreats
Among the din of noisy streets,
In rooms with faded drapes,
To look from wicker chairs
And see the slums the years had made
Of what was once an aspen glade
For Baptist picnics, county fairs.

On Looking Into a Wedding Album

I

This picture shows the room,
The "eloquence" of white,
The youthful bride and groom.

(In later years they'd mock
That "Diane Arbus" pose,
That gawky pair in shock.)

"These kids know how to live,"
The tippling priest declared,
"With so much love to give."

New lovers never sense
An hour when love might wane,
Their passion's so intense.

II

With time her auburn hair
Presages grey, his eyes
Assume a somber air.

Were we like that? they muse,
Who every passing year
Have less and less to lose.

They find they've spent their lives
Lamenting all that's gone,
Neglecting what survives.

New lovers never dream
What Heraclitus knew,
That life's a shifting stream.

III

As light began to fade
They posed for this last shot
Along a balustrade.

They stood and waved farewell
To relatives and friends,
Intent on some hotel.

Tomorrow loomed ahead
Across the far off hills,
To cherish, not to dread.

Whatever lies in store,
New lovers always know
Their love's forevermore.

Lilith

Those eyes, so lovely then,
Could cast a winding skein
To trap unwary men.

Abstracted by those eyes,
I lingered night and day,
Believing all her lies.

And when, in her ennui,
She let me slip away,
I still was never free.

I sense my second fall,
When summer's leaves begin
Their dark recessional.

I scream her name alone
In throes of restless sleep,
A hunger in the bone.

The Child Left Alone in a Storm

I think of what you felt that night
When winter beat upon the door
And gusts of wind blew out the light,
A fear like none you'd known before,
Forgotten child, who woke alone,
The others in the family gone.

You heard the surge from down the stairs,
The blast that echoed through the wall,
The crackling timbers, creaking chairs
Erupting in the parlor, hall,
That complement of boards and wind
Unsettling a young girl's mind.

Awakening with no one there,
What god or saint could you implore?
What children's voices raised in prayer
forestall a storm outside the door?
The panic racing through your head,
You filled the night with screams instead.

A Christmas Ghost

As seasonal as sentiment,
He comes around this time of year,
That querulous old revenant.

I've thrown away his letters, notes,
Mislaid his faded photographs,
Forgotten all his anecdotes.

"Just wait," he warns. "You'll see the day,
Perhaps before your body's cold,
Your own effects are tossed away."

The children long for Christmas Eve,
The presents underneath the tree
They wait for unseen hands to leave.

We sit around the radio,
Hear "Silver Bells" and "Silent Night,"
Reflect about the chance of snow.

"You'll know the truth the week you die,"
The bitter voice of Christmas drones.
I've learned to turn the volume high.

Femmes Fatale

For a Voluptuary

With Paolo and Francesca doomed to spin
In swirling air for one pathetic sin,
I contemplate the cataclysmic gust
That waits to punish our prodigious lust.

To a Miss California Contestant,
Disqualified for Appearing Nude on the Internet

You played the beauty to the core,
But beauty is so quickly frayed,
It's often worn away before
The echoes of its praises fade.

To a Diva

Vorrei e non vorrei, you said
Then slipped at once inside my bed.

For a Three Named Lady Poet

Accept this ash, the last remains
Of all your *billet-doux*,
And sing, for once, no sad refrains.

For notes professing love, desire,
(What metaphors you drew!)
They made a rather paltry fire.

Pressed Flowers

As though, despite the toll of age,
These blooms made passion reappear,
You show me, tucked inside a page,
The flowers I gave you late last year.
If love could last as long as flowers
You press in books on summer days,
These wouldn't be our final hours,
We needn't go our separate ways.
We've watched this spent affair drag on
Though seasons change and flowers turn,
And color, fragrance fade, are gone.
We've learned what other lovers learn:
Of all the flowers that bloom at night
How few will last through morning light.

III
Consolations

We'll shut our eyes against the wind and rain,
And waking, we'll arise and build again.

Apparitions

A perfect logic rules our dreams
From swaddling clothes to winding sheet,
And urges me — turned twelve again —
To climb among the glowing boughs

Of phosphorescent apples trees,
Endow equivocating leaves
With apparitions formed anew
Beneath that orchard's halfway moon.

I scramble to the utmost limb,
Survey the things that lie below,
A landscape so familiar once,
It seems more real to me than life.

Was I that boy of spells and charms
Who watched a dazzling world unfold
Beneath those godsend summer skies?
Who saw such wondrous things in leaves,

Those figures etched in rain-streaked
Walls, the silver tracery of clouds,
Those varied splendors, changing shapes
Each place I set my drowsy eyes?

Doorish

For Elizabeth Carnazzo

I

A rundown Georgian house,
The remnants of a barn,
A stony plot of fallow ground —
It took a Connachtman
To give this place a name,
Some farmer, kin of mine,
Who plowed and harrowed here
Two hundred years ago or more,
Who knew the cradle maker's skill,
The coffin builder's art.

II

I tell the dowager
Who gives me tea and cake
I've come to her from far away,
Walked miles of country road
To find this humble farm.

She speaks distractedly
Of Simpsons, Martins, all
That Church of Ireland crowd
(The rusty kettle, long forgot,
Still steaming on the hob),

The ones who stayed behind,
Her relatives and mine.
They sleep in country churchyards now,
Their graves almost concealed
With sprawling ivy, weeds.

I think of uncles, aunts
Who sat on Brooklyn stoops
Before the two World Wars and longed
For seed and harvest times in fields
They never saw again.

III

At dusk I take my leave
Of every stick and stone
Of generations island proud,
Whose industry sustained these fields,
Replenished fallow ground.

The cradle maker's heir,
The coffin builder's kin,
I wander back along the road,
With neither skill nor art to raise
These ruins up again.

Summer Snow

I

Those winters at my uncle's lodge
Are pallid childhood memories,
Except her vivid face, that face
I saw just once when I was eight.

Returning from the slopes one day,
I shivered by a blazing fire.
Two girls I'd never seen approached.
"Been sledding through the snow?" one asked,

A stunning girl of twelve or so
With long black hair and deep blue eyes.
"I bet you're freezing cold," she purred.
I lied, a quaver in my voice.

"You haven't found the summer snow beyond
The ridge?" she asked. "There's drifts and drifts.
It's warm and cozy there. You just lie down
And let it cover you; it's dreamy stuff."

Her silent friend exchanged a look with her.
"I guess we have to go," she said. "Goodbye,
But don't forget those drifts of summer snow.
Perhaps we'll see you there sometime."

II

A blaze destroyed my uncle's lodge
Next autumn, when it didn't rain.
Although we didn't know it then,
We'd spent our final winter there.

What slopes I see these days appear
In dreams of summits far away.
I pull my sled across that ridge,
Still seeking drifts of summer snow.

My Grandmother Spoke of Cranes

In memory of Katherine Teresa Sherman

A flock of whooping cranes surprised her once,
Descending from below a bank of clouds
In Canada a century ago,
When she was young, a prairie farmer's wife.

They soared by overhead above the barn
And then across Alberta's golden plains.
"I still can hear their call," she told me late
In life, mistaking me for Fred, her son.

Of granite stock, she lived through storm and drought,
And bore her first live child alone, then took
The infant, wrapped in wool, across the miles
Of icy drifts to show her startled spouse.

Around Alberta then, most people thought
It lucky to observe a single crane.
She'd seen a flock above the barn that day,
A mass of white against an azure sky.

They sold the struggling farm and moved before
The power lines were hung, the marshlands drained.
If carcasses were strewn across those plains,
Well, God gave man dominion over fowl.

Not much is left of those Alberta days
When women worked in fields beside their men
And flights of whooping cranes passed overhead
In skies, she swore, were somehow bluer then.

The Monaghans

They'd scour the countryside
To find some grassy bed,
The lissome girl beneath,
The tousled boy astride.

We'd see them after dark,
Her hair of palest oak
Espalliered among leaves
In meadow, field and park.

Until grey-fingered days
Brought righteous wind and rain,
No patch of ground was spared
These amorous forays.

That hair has gone to snow
From shades of palest oak;
For years a vital man,
Arthritis brought him low.

So freighted with the years
They rarely venture out,
How odd they both suggest
This latter love is best.

Reflections in a County Kerry Churchyard

What these departed want is to be invited back,
To move into their old rooms, sleep
In their beds, wear their Sunday best again.

They miss the carouses of summer nights,
The winter evenings warmed by fires,
The clocks ticking the change of seasons.

They long for pantomimes, games,
The tunes played on a tinkling piano,
The intimate frolics of the small hours.

Following the solemn rites of farewell,
Their clothes were bundled and sent away,
Their pictures weathered in desk drawers.

In sleep we hear them calling in the distance,
Standing alone on empty platforms,
Waiting for trains that never arrive.

Elegy For a Minor Shakespearian Actor

His Antony before the war
The *Guardian* pronounced a bore.
The *Times* declared his Prospero
Was better twenty years ago.
His histrionics playing Lear
His fellow actors couldn't hear.

I see him now in grave repose
In clothes his loyal dresser chose.
What some have called his stony brow
Seems calm and understated now.
Those flailing arms, for once at rest,
Impart the somber subtext best.

Though never one to grace the stage
With comic wit, heroic rage,
He'll fill a walk-off part today,
The final role all actors play.
Too bad he lacks the wherewithal
To take a final curtain call.

The Late Humanitarian

The institutes that bear his name,
Presumptive Bauhaus, never brick,
Have strayed from his *Principia*
(Of course he always knew they would).

He saw that hunger, war, disease
Would prove to be indigenous;
That ignorance might make extinct
That most endangered species, man.

Aware his stores of love and light
Would barely serve to strike a line
From all the rolls of human want,
He wrung his hands and persevered.

The urchins scrawl obscenities
Across his bronze memorials,
The cenotaphs in public squares
(Of course he always knew they would).

Another Bloomsday at Molly Malone's Pub

And didn't we have the curious time
That night with the cuckolds and the muckers
(Alive, alive, ha!),
Bloom moldy for a pint
Like the plain papal of Ireland.

The gleesome lad and friends,
Mimers and mummers all,
Out-Joycing Joyce
In the dark and smoky rheum.
Ineluctable modality of the voluble.

Mac grievous, the Juman himself,
With his leer and his dank knickers,
And lassome Gerty on the strand:
Erin go braless
With pink ribboned drawers.

And Molly Manybeaus, as in the
Begatting, word without end,
Going on about her private arts
Till Barney, Jem and Dosser
Were wanking their way home.

And those fiddlers and singers, Guild
men and true, twittering
Monto and Love's Oul
Sweet Sin as that pride
Of sloothering drunks bellied for more.

God bliss us and salve us,
Who said buggers can't be chancers?
But riddle me this, if you can
My foin finicky scalder,
Except for the scribbler in the corner

With his jar and his long face
(Night of the doleful countenance),
Which of those claptomaniacs
Opened or closed a book
By Seamus Joyce in his life?

Memento, Ergo Sum

You know nothing of the past, you have dreamt it.
O.V. de L. Milosz, L'Etrangere

In dreams they catch my eye on public streets,
Those skulking men and women, hail me, call
My name aloud, refuse to let me pass.
They knew me once on Scott or Lincoln Roads,
When I was six, or eight, or ten years old.

Perhaps they were at school with me or worked
The same dull summer gig when we were teens.
I can't ignore the ever present grin,
The restive way they fix their eyes on me.
I smile at them and hardly say a word.

My lapse, of course, prolongs their talk, until
I realize I've missed the bus or plane
I booked to some forgotten terminus,
While they describe a boy I don't recall,
A man I never met in all those years.

Is what these dream tormentors claim the truth?
And what is truth? Did Plato ever say?
Does Death, that seasoned arbiter, decide?
They're waiting in the dark out there tonight,
And all I have is memory to ward them off.

All Souls

Christopher S. Kerrigan
(b. 1983)
Christopher Thompson
(1944-1972)

Beneath his cerement of reeds
That twilight spirit stirs again,
Emerging from those depths,
The waters where he drowned,
To bear a child across the void.

Conceived within an inner dark,
We long for archetypal night,
We contemplate like voyagers
Our passages from shore to shore.
May ages gather voices there.

Insistent bells commemorate
A brother dead, a namesake son.
These icons, candles signify
Our florid articles of faith,
Our sacred pilgrimage of blood.

We mourn a fallen son and heir
(Submerged anew among those reeds
Till time shall raise him up again),
In water, which engenders all,
We celebrate an infant boy.

Dublin: Autumn Dusk

The clock above the Irish Times
Forswearing the faltered day,

A slathering mist on the hills,

A gaffer outside O'Neal's
Afflicting passing strangers
With the secrets of his arid age,

A flurry of gulls on the Liffey,

The bridges drifting into a night
As nebulous as the unraveled day,

A crone beckoning to death
Across the dark water
With frail and brittle gestures,

The massive head of O'Connell
Brooding on his vision of a city,

The heavy air sinking
As darkness palls the quays.

Dublin Streets in Winter

Facades of grey in Georgian streets,
In Dublin, unfamiliar then.
The summer tourists all gone home,
McDonough, Pearse, McBride, et al.
Returned to skulk about the streets
With seething rancor, cold remorse.

Another twenty years have passed,
You hear outside the fanlight rows
That litany of old disputes.
A city gone to seed, renewed,
Her lovers stroll in Stephens Green,
Her statues ponder grey defeats.

The kindred generations pass
Along the banks of both canals
As darkness falls on city parks,
On bridges, chapels, monuments.
Within its freight of swans and filth
The ambling Liffey fashions myths.

The gargle flows as freely still,
You sit in dim ancestral pubs
In Baggot Street or Eden Quay
And hear the drinkers' chronic talk.
The voices from the darkness speak
With seething rancor, cold remorse.

Dublin 1966, 1986

Elegy For a Stage Actress

I always thought we'd meet again one day,
With you in pink or purple *crepe de Chine.*
We'd have a glass or two of Chardonnay,
Perhaps discuss the local drama scene.
Instead, I sit inside a dive alone
Off Fuller Street and nurse a Black and White,
A place with just a single telephone,
But then I won't be calling you tonight.
For you there's no Millennium, no chance
To rectify your failings down the years,
Not even one more free for all romance,
No falling out, no last display of tears,
For Death's a leading man you can't upstage,
Who lent the boards such passion once, such rage.

Hollywood, 1999

Odalisque

She could have been an odalisque
Who posed for Ingres or Delacroix,
He thought, that afternoon he saw
Her standing in the *Place Michel.*

Among the crowds of passersby
He'd seen in wanton Paris days
En route to nearby bars, cafes,
He'd come upon no face like hers.

His frail disguise of nonchalance
Dissolved upon their first embrace.
She took his fingers, helped him trace
The deep defile between her breasts.

The hour they spent at some hotel
Outside of *St. Germain des Pres*
Was all they had, and yet, that day
He witnessed beauty unadorned,

Beheld, before she brushed aside
Her chestnut hair, and rose to dress,
The spoil a sultan might possess.
She could have been an odalisque.

Daughters

For Leda, Katherine, Hilary, and Elizabeth

You emerge auspiciously on the planet,
The strangers we crafted in darkness,
Wearing the bodies we provided
(Fashioned so they fit you perfectly).

You crawl happily at our feet,
Our fair supplanters on the earth,
In that new and perfect flesh.

One day you surprise us as women,
Waiting for our astonished approval
As though you had done a flip or a handspring.

Listen to me for once, my progeny,
Already time is beginning
To turn its back on your father.

I speak to you in the words of a man
Obscured by the gathering shadows —
Fall in love wisely,
Bear children like yourselves.

A Sighting

I

That summer morning years ago
We saw a red-tailed hawk
Descending from some pines
Across this scroll of riverbed.

His talons clutching writhing prey,
His plumage spread against
A shaft of swirling air,
We saw him slowly rise again.

That circling image calls us back
As strangers now, to drift
Beneath these trees, this sky,
To wonder where the river leads.

We tie our rotting skiff along
A fringe of wooded shore,
Survey a massive sky
For hours for pinions, talons, beak.

II

A vagrant sun recedes behind
A line of reddened hills.
At dusk, let down and cold,
We slowly row the skiff downstream,
Then make our way to camp as night
Reclaims the river, pines.

Without a word exchanged
We pack the old sedan and leave.

We saw a sign among these woods
That morning years ago,
An emblematic bird
Abreast of water, earth and sky.

If we can hoard its symmetry
Against the whorl of time,
Perhaps it was enough
To know that feathered splendor once.

Coole Park Revisited

Among what rushes will they build,
By what lake's edge or pool
Delight man's eyes when I awake some day
To find they have flown away.

W.B. Yeats, The Wild Swans at Coole

I

"So many lovely things are gone,"
You said, those brooding latter days.
At Coole, a Georgian manor house
Played host to genius down the years,
A country's poets, playwrights, wits,
But blackguard time would pull it down.
Just up the road the Martyn heirs
Contrived to lose Tyllira House;
And who ascends your winding stair
At Ballylee but tourists now?

II

Returning to these Seven Woods,
I leave the world of ghosts awhile.
I go to find those swans again
That wheel and dive across the lake,
Near kin of those you ventured once
Were emblems of the human soul.
What's lost, preserved in years to come
No man can ever prophesy.
Will sylphlike swans be gliding here
When men are silent, man extinct?

Storms

For Sean Kerrigan

When days of stormy skies have done their worst,
And river waters rise and levees burst;
When men implore their gods as skies grow dark,
And every two-by-four becomes an ark;
When friends are lost and burdened with our grief,
We count the cost of storms with disbelief;
When children doubt and wonder how we'll live
And we're without assurances to give;
When we're bereft of all, except the dross,
And mankind's left to calculate its loss;
We'll shut our eyes against the wind and rain,
And waking, we'll arise and build again.

September, 2005

The Dust of Stars

For Louis Turenne

Time was, men breathed the dust of stars,
The smoke from long exploded worlds
When chaos shook the galaxy.
Their voices made the rocks resound
With music never heard before.
To pacify the jealous gods,
They played upon the three-stringed lyre
And gave an antiphon to man.
But science wished their music stilled.
Philosophy would deem them mad,
And some proposed to drive their kind
Beyond the city gates en masse,
Those men of dialectic mind
Who never breathed the dust of stars.

Notes

14 The lyrics are from *Carmen.*

22 "Ó Ciaragáin" (Kerrigan) means "of the dark people."

25 The phrase "windy stool" means windowsill.

27 The reference to being brought down by "Huns" is an allusion to Goethe's statement that the Irish seemed to him like a pack of hounds dragging down a noble stag.

34 This was written for the birth announcement of a daughter.

48 The poem is a parody of Leigh Hunt's *Jenny Kissed Me.*

60 Michael Praetorius mistakenly thought the word "concerto" was derived from the Latin "contendere" (to "contend").

66 Rilke did, indeed, die as a result of pricking a finger on a rose thorn.

84 Doorish is the name of a farm in Coolaney, County Sligo, the home of my grandmother.

98 MacDonagh, Pearse, and McBride were participants in the Easter rising of 1916 in Dublin.

Printed in the United States
109068LV00002B/181-249/P

9 780979 845208